THE BEST 50
BERRIES RECIPES

Joanna White

BRISTOL PUBLISHING ENTERPRISES
San Leandro, California

Printed in the United States of America.

ISBN 1-55867-160-9

Cover design: Frank J. Paredes
Cover photography: John A Benson
Food stylist: Merilee Hague Bordin

BERRY BASICS

Berries are usually associated with summertime. Some varieties, such as strawberries, are now available year-round because of fast transportation from warmer climates. Many types of berries are available in the frozen section of your local grocery store. Besides being made into jams, jellies, preserves and syrups, berries can be used fresh in salads or drinks, made into sauces for entrées and desserts, or baked into breads, scones, cookies, muffins, cakes and pies. Generally, berries are high in vitamin C and minerals and low in calories. Open your mind to the wonderful world of berries.

EQUIVALENTS

- 1 lb. berries equals approximately 4 cups.
- 1 flat weighs approximately 6 lb., which is enough filling for 3 pies, or approximately 10 jars (8 oz. each) jam.

CHOOSING BERRIES

- Choose firm, ripe, juicy berries with even color.
- Avoid buying baskets that are stained. It usually means that berries are overripe and soft.
- Avoid berries that are shriveled and appear dull. Look for plump berries with shiny skins.
- Avoid berries with green or white tops, or blemishes.
- For optimum flavor, eat berries at room temperature.

STORAGE AND HANDLING

- Wash berries by placing them in a colander and rinsing gently under a spray of cold water. Dry berries by gently rolling them on a towel or paper towels. Never soak berries in water. Wash strawberries before hulling so they will not absorb water.

- Remove any moldy berries immediately. One bad berry can spoil the whole group.
- Refrigerate and use most berries within 2 days. Gooseberries and blueberries last for up to a week in the refrigerator. Remove berries from their container, arrange them in a single layer in a shallow pan lined with paper towels and cover them with plastic wrap.
- To freeze berries, line a baking sheet with waxed paper and arrange berries in a single layer so they don't touch. Place berries, uncovered, flat in the freezer for about 2 hours, or until frozen. Transfer berries to a nonmetallic, moistureproof container. Remove as much air as possible before sealing. Place the container in the freezer for up to 1 year. Strawberries should be washed, hulled and sliced before placing in a locking freezer bag with a little sugar. They tend to discolor and collapse when frozen whole.

VARIETIES

Blackberry: dark-purple, velvet-like. Varies in size. Many hybrids. High in calcium and vitamin B1. Available: mid-June through July.

Blueberry: dark purplish-blue, round, varies in size. Many types. Available: late June through September.

Boysenberry: deep maroon, large and plump with a tart, perfumy flavor. Available: early June through mid-August.

Cranberry: round, red, firm and quite tart. Usually needs sugar when cooking. Cooking yields much juice. High in vitamin A. Available: October through December.

Gooseberry: crunchy, sour, light green or rose-colored when ripe. Available: June and sometimes into mid-July.

Huckleberry: small, round blueberry, delicious and sweet when ripe. Some varieties are red. Available: mid-June through Labor Day.

Lingonberry: small, bright red, round, commonly found in Scandinavia and Alaska. Available: late August through September.

Loganberry: deep reddish-maroon, cone-shaped, tart. Flavor is a cross between a blackberry and raspberry. Available: mid-May through mid-July.

Marionberry: cross between a wild and domestic blackberry. Medium-sized, slightly elongated with a unique tangy-sweet flavor. Contains few seeds. Ideal for pies. Available: mid-July through mid-August.

Nectarberry: large, deep burgundy, sweet with a slight floral taste. Available: mid-July through mid-August.

Olallieberry: medium to large cultivated blackberry hybrid. Slender, shiny, black. Available: late May through early July.

Raspberry: red is the most common variety and when ripe is quite sweet. Black variety is small and seedy with a mild tart flavor. Gold type is a little sweeter and milder than red. Early-bearing raspberries are available mid-May through June. Late-bearing raspberries are available mid-July through December.

Strawberry: white to bright red to deep scarlet. Heart-shaped. Wild (smaller) variety is very fragrant and sweet. Available: July through September.

Tayberry: scarlet red, cone-shaped, cross between a blackberry and raspberry. Quite tart. Very good mixed with other berries. Available: mid-June through mid-July.

BLUEBERRY MUFFINS

These morning favorites are made special with mace.

3 cups flour
4 tsp. baking powder
½ tsp. salt
1 cup sugar
½ tsp. mace or nutmeg
2 cups fresh or frozen
  blueberries, patted dry

2 eggs, beaten
¼ cup butter, melted
1 cup milk
grated peel (zest) of 2 lemons
warmed honey for glaze,
  optional

Preheat oven to 400°. In a bowl, mix together flour, baking powder, salt, sugar and mace. Stir in berries. Stir together eggs, butter, milk and peel. Combine mixtures just to blend and spoon into greased or paper-lined muffin cups. Bake for 20 to 25 minutes. Remove to a baking rack to cool. If desired, brush with a little warm honey.

Makes: 30 muffins

CRANBERRY CHEESE BREAD

Surprisingly, cheese enhances the cranberry flavor and adds richness to this wonderful, moist bread.

4 cups flour
2 cups sugar
1 tbs. baking powder
1 tsp. salt
1 tsp. baking soda
2 tbs. grated fresh orange peel (zest)
1/4 cup butter, cut into pieces
3 cups grated cheddar cheese
1/2 cup orange juice
2 eggs
2 cups chopped cranberries

Preheat oven to 350°. Line the bottom of 2 loaf pans with brown paper and grease paper and sides well. In a bowl, mix together flour, sugar, baking powder, salt, baking soda and orange peel. With a pastry blender or 2 knives, cut in butter until mixture resembles small peas. Stir in cheddar cheese. Beat orange juice and eggs together and stir into flour mixture. Gently stir in cranberries. Pour into prepared loaf pans and bake for 60 to 65 minutes or until a knife inserted in the center comes out clean. Cool for 15 minutes. Turn out onto racks to cool completely.

Makes: 2 loaves

BLUEBERRY BUCKLE

This variation on coffeecake has a streusel topping that is drenched in lemon sauce and broiled. It's great served warm as a rich breakfast treat, or for dessert.

½ cup butter, softened
1½ cups sugar
2 eggs, beaten
1 cup milk
4 cups flour

4 tsp. baking powder
1 tsp. salt
1¼ tsp. cinnamon
2 cups blueberries

Preheat oven to 375°. Beat butter and sugar together until light and creamy. Add eggs and milk and mix well. Mix together flour, baking powder, salt and cinnamon. Add to butter mixture and stir to combine. Gently fold in blueberries and pour into a greased 9-x-13-inch pan.

TOPPING

½ cup butter, cut into pieces
1 cup sugar

⅔ cup flour
½ tsp. mace or nutmeg

Combine topping ingredients until crumbly and sprinkle evenly over batter. Bake for 45 minutes or until done.

SAUCE

1 cup butter
2 cups sugar
2½ cups water
2 eggs, beaten

⅓ cup lemon juice
3 tbs. grated fresh lemon peel
(zest)

Preheat broiler. Melt butter in a saucepan. Add sugar, water and eggs. Bring to a boil. Remove from heat and stir in lemon juice and lemon peel. Pour over baked cake and broil until bubbly and golden. Cut into squares to serve.

Servings: 12

STRAWBERRY TEA BREAD

This is a wonderful bread to serve with honey butter for a tea.

3 cups flour
2 cups sugar
1 tsp. baking powder
1½ cups chopped toasted
   pecans
1 tsp. salt
1 tbs. cinnamon

4 eggs, beaten
1¼ cups butter, melted
2 pkg. (10 oz. each) frozen
   strawberries, thawed, or
   3 cups chopped fresh
   strawberries

Preheat oven to 350°. Line 2 greased loaf pans with greased brown paper. Stir together flour, sugar, baking powder, pecans, salt and cinnamon. Stir in eggs and butter until well mixed. Stir in berries. Pour into prepared pans and bake for 1 hour or until bread tests done. Cool in pan for 10 minutes. Turn out onto a rack to cool completely.

Makes: 2 loaves

BLUEBERRY COFFEECAKE

This breakfast or snack cake is best served warm.

2/3 cup butter, softened
1 cup sugar
3 eggs, separated
3 cups flour
1 tbs. baking powder
1/4 tsp. salt

1/4 tsp. mace or nutmeg
1 cup milk or buttermilk
2 cups fresh or frozen
    blueberries
1/3 cup brown sugar, packed

Preheat oven to 375°. Beat butter with sugar until fluffy. Add yolks and beat until creamy. Mix together flour, baking powder, salt and mace. Add to butter mixture alternately with milk, mixing until smooth. Gently stir in blueberries. Beat egg whites to stiff peaks and fold into batter. Pour into a greased 9-inch square pan and sprinkle with brown sugar. Bake for 35 minutes or until done.

Servings: 9

MIXED BERRY BREAD PUDDING

*Berry bread pudding makes a great breakfast treat. It's also good
for dessert served in a pool of raspberry sauce and garnished
with whipped cream. Egg bread has the best flavor and texture
for bread puddings. Use raspberries, blackberries, blueberries,
strawberries or another variety.*

1 qt. milk
1 cup sugar
½ tsp. nutmeg
pinch cinnamon
2 tsp. vanilla extract
6 eggs, beaten
6 cups cubed egg bread (1-inch cubes)
¼ cup butter, melted
4 cups mixed berries
Raspberry Sauce, follows

Preheat broiler. In a saucepan, bring milk to a boil and remove from heat. Add sugar, nutmeg and cinnamon and stir to combine. Cool. Beat in vanilla and eggs; set aside. Toss bread cubes in melted butter, place on a baking sheet and toast under the broiler. Reduce heat to 350°. Place bread cubes in a buttered 3-quart baking dish and spoon berries on top. Pour milk mixture over bread and bake for 1 hour or until custard is set. Serve with *Raspberry Sauce*.

RASPBERRY SAUCE

2 cups fresh or frozen raspberries
2 tbs. confectioners' sugar, or to taste
2-3 drops framboise or kirsch, optional

Puree all ingredients with a food processor or blender until smooth. Strain through a sieve to remove seeds. Taste and adjust sweetness.

Servings: 12

SWEDISH PANCAKES WITH LINGONBERRIES

*If you can't find fresh lingonberries, use lingonberry jam. Combine 1½ cups jam with 2 cups softened butter for a variation of **Lingonberry Butter**. Dilute and heat the jam for a variation of **Lingonberry Syrup**.*

PANCAKES

6 eggs
2½ cups whole milk
1½ cups flour

2 tbs. sugar
1 tsp. salt

Blend all ingredients until smooth. Pour a small amount of batter (enough to coat the bottom of pan thinly) into a hot, greased 12-inch skillet. Brown pancake over medium heat for about 1 minute. Turn and cook for 30 seconds. Serve immediately with *Lingonberry Butter* and/or *Lingonberry Syrup*.

Servings: 6

LINGONBERRY BUTTER

1½ cups fresh lingonberries   ½ cup sugar
¼ cup water   2 cups butter, softened

Place lingonberries and water in a saucepan and cook over medium heat until berries are soft. Stir in sugar until dissolved and remove from heat. Puree mixture and cool. Mix well with butter and refrigerate.

Makes: 3½ cups

LINGONBERRY SYRUP

1 lb. lingonberries   ¼ cup sugar, or to taste
½ cup water   pinch cinnamon, optional
1 tsp. fresh lemon juice

Cook lingonberries in water over medium heat until berries are soft. Stir in remaining ingredients. If desired, puree mixture until smooth.

Makes: 2½ cups

BASIC BERRY SOUP

This basic recipe can be used with most fresh or frozen berries. Apple juice, instead of sugar, sweetens it naturally. Consider this as a light dessert served with a scoop of ice cream or frozen yogurt. Use blueberries, raspberries, blackberries or another variety.

1 pt. berries
3½ cups water
2 cups apple juice
¼ tsp. salt
⅛ tsp. nutmeg, mace or cinnamon
sugar to taste
2 tbs. cornstarch
2 tbs. cold water
¼ cup fresh lemon juice
whipped cream for garnish, optional

Place berries and water in a saucepan and bring to a boil. Simmer for 20 minutes or until berries are soft. Push mixture through a sieve to remove seeds, return to saucepan and add apple juice, salt, nutmeg and sugar. Mix cornstarch with cold water and stir into berry mixture. Stir constantly over medium heat until mixture thickens and clears. Remove from heat and chill. Stir in lemon juice, taste and adjust seasonings. Serve chilled and, if desired, garnish with a dollop of whipped cream.

VARIATION: CREAMY BERRY SOUP

Add 1 cup sour cream and beat until smooth.

Servings: 6

TANGY RASPBERRY SOUP

You can also serve this as a sauce for a platter of fruit.

1½ tbs. unflavored gelatin
⅓ cup cold water
¾ cup hot water
4½ cups fresh raspberries, or 3 pkg. (10 oz. each) frozen raspberries, thawed
1½ cups pineapple juice

1⅓ cups dry sherry
⅓ cup grenadine
2 tbs. fresh lemon juice
1 cup half-and-half
3½ cups sour cream or yogurt
sugar or honey to taste, optional

In a saucepan, soften gelatin in cold water for 5 minutes. Add hot water and stir over medium heat until gelatin dissolves. Cool. Puree raspberries with a food processor or blender. Strain to remove seeds. Mix berries with all ingredients, whisking until smooth. Chill for several hours before serving.

Servings: 12

STRAWBERRY-ORANGE SOUP

This appetizer soup has just a hint of spices, but you can add more.

3 pt. fresh strawberries, hulled,
   reserve 6 for garnish
1½ cups orange juice
2 tsp. instant tapioca
⅛ tsp. cinnamon
pinch ground allspice
pinch ground cardamom

¾ cup sugar
1 tbs. grated fresh lemon peel
   (zest)
1½ tsp. lemon juice
1½ cups buttermilk
1 orange, thinly sliced for
   garnish

Puree berries and pour into a saucepan. Add orange juice, tapioca and spices. Heat, stirring constantly, until mixture comes to a boil; reduce heat and simmer until thickened. Remove from heat and stir in sugar, lemon peel, lemon juice and buttermilk. Chill for several hours. Garnish with orange slices and quartered strawberries.

Makes 6 servings.

BLUEBERRY-PEACH FROZEN SALAD

*Serve this salad on a plate of lettuce with a side of **Blueberry Cream Dressing**, page 29, if desired.*

3 oz. cream cheese, softened
1 tbs. lemon juice
⅛ tsp. salt
⅓ cup sugar
1 cup diced canned peaches, well drained

1 cup fresh blueberries
1 pt. sour cream (can use low-fat or nonfat)
fresh blueberries and peaches for garnish, optional

Stir together cream cheese, lemon juice, salt and sugar until smooth. Gently fold in peaches, blueberries and sour cream. Line a loaf pan or mold with waxed paper and pour in mixture. Freeze until firm. Slice and serve on a bed of lettuce, garnished with blueberries and peaches, if desired.

Servings: 4

CRANBERRY-PINEAPPLE SALAD

Make this salad the day before you serve it to allow the flavors to meld. It's a great salad any time of the year.

1 pkg. (12 oz.) fresh or frozen cranberries
1¼ cups sugar
2 cups whipping cream
2 cups miniature marshmallows
8 oz. crushed pineapple, drained

With a food processor or blender, process cranberries and sugar until berries are coarsely chopped. Place in a large bowl and refrigerate for 2 hours. Whip cream and fold into remaining ingredients along with cranberries. Cover and refrigerate overnight.

Servings: 8

EXOTIC BERRY SALAD

Red onions, yellow fruit and a colorful variety of berries on a bed of greens make a beautiful presentation. For the lettuce, use Bibb, romaine, leaf, watercress or another variety. A tasty raspberry vinaigrette complements this salad nicely. Garnish with peppery nasturtium flowers if desired.

2 heads lettuce
1 small red onion, thinly sliced
2-3 mangoes, sliced into long wedges
2-3 oranges, peeled and sectioned
1 pt. mixed berries (marionberries, blackberries, raspberries, blueberries or another variety)
$\frac{1}{2}$ cup toasted sliced almonds
stemmed nasturtium flowers for garnish, optional

Wash, dry and tear lettuce into bite-sized pieces and place on individual plates or a large serving platter. Sprinkle red onions over lettuce and artfully arrange mangoes, oranges and berries on top. Sprinkle with almonds and garnish with flowers, if using. Serve drizzled with dressing.

Servings: 6-8

DRESSING

1½ cups olive oil
½ cup raspberry vinegar
1-2 tbs. sugar
salt and pepper to taste

Blend all ingredients. Taste and adjust seasonings.

Makes: 2 cups

FRESH FRUIT WITH STRAWBERRY-GINGER DRESSING

Garnish this delicious salad with fresh mint.

2 tbs. chopped crystallized
    ginger
1 tbs. brown sugar, packed
1 medium banana, peeled
1 tbs. rum, or more to taste
2½ cups strawberries, sliced
1 cup sour cream

1 pt. fresh blueberries or other
    berries
2 cups sliced bananas
1 cup peeled and chopped
    peaches, mangoes or
    papayas (prefer fresh)

Process ginger and brown sugar with a food processor until ginger is finely chopped. Add banana, rum and ½ cup of the strawberries and process until smooth. Add sour cream and mix well. Place remaining fruit in a bowl and toss with dressing. Chill.

Servings: 6

POPPY SEED DRESSING

Serve this dressing over fresh fruit salads. It goes especially well with a salad of spinach, strawberries, avocados and toasted nuts. Substitute olive, corn, peanut or another mild-tasting oil.

2 cups vegetable oil
2/3 cup cider vinegar
1 1/2 cups sugar
3 tbs. finely chopped white onion
1/4 cup poppy seeds
2 tsp. dry mustard
2 tsp. salt

Blend all ingredients with a food processor or blender. Taste and adjust seasonings. Keep refrigerated.

Makes: 4 cups

BERRY VINAIGRETTE

Get out of your rut and try a new vinaigrette! This is great served on a salad of mixed greens and berries, or drizzled over fresh fruit. Substitute olive, corn, peanut or any mild-tasting oil. Raspberries and blackberries work well, but you can use any type.

3 tbs. vegetable oil
1 tbs. red wine vinegar
1 tsp. salt, or to taste
¼ tsp. pepper

1 tsp. Dijon mustard
1½-2 cups fresh or frozen
   berries
sugar to taste, optional

In a bowl, mix together oil, vinegar, salt, pepper and mustard. Puree berries with a food processor or blender and push through a fine strainer to remove seeds (should make about 1 cup pulp). Mix pulp into oil and vinegar mixture and sweeten if desired.

Makes: 1½ cups

BLUEBERRY CREAM DRESSING

This dressing is great on fruit salads or as a dip on a fruit platter.
Huckleberries or blackberries can be substituted for the
blueberries if desired.

½ cup crushed blueberries
1 tbs. lemon juice
2 tbs. sugar
pinch salt
1 cup sour cream (can use nonfat or low-fat)

Mix blueberries, lemon juice, sugar and salt together until well
blended. Fold in sour cream and chill until ready to serve.

Makes: 1½ cups

RASPBERRY YOGURT DRESSING

Serve this as a dip for fresh fruit. Don't limit yourself to raspberries — this recipe also works for blackberries, blueberries and strawberries. You may have to adjust the amount of honey depending on the tartness of the berries.

1 cup low-fat plain or fruit yogurt
1 cup low-fat cottage cheese
1 cup fresh raspberries
2 tbs. honey, or to taste
1 tbs. raspberry vinegar

Place all ingredients in a food processor or blender container and process until smooth. Taste and adjust sweetness. If desired, strain mixture through a sieve to remove seeds. Keep refrigerated until ready to use.

Makes: 3 cups

SALMON WITH BERRY SAUCE

This sauce is also good on roast chicken and duck.

1½ cups fresh blackberries,
   loganberries or marionberries
⅓-½ cup sugar
½ cup water
2 tbs. lemon juice

1 jar (6 oz.) hoisin sauce
pepper to taste
6 salmon fillets, 6 oz. each
olive oil for brushing

Preheat oven to 500°. In a saucepan, cook berries with sugar and water until berries are soft, about 20 minutes. Puree mixture and press through a sieve. Stir in lemon juice, hoisin sauce and pepper. Sear fillets in a very hot, ovenproof skillet (prefer cast iron) for 1 minute on each side. Remove from heat and brush fillets with olive oil. Spoon on berry sauce and bake for about 7 minutes, or until fish is cooked through. Serve immediately.

Servings: 6

CRANBERRY CORNISH HENS

Cranberries are a perfect complement to fowl dishes. Add orange juice and pecans, and you have a superb combination that will keep eaters coming back for more. Use unseasoned bread cubes.

1 can (8 oz.), whole berry
   cranberry sauce, or 1½ cups
   Classic Cranberry Sauce,
   page 37
2 tbs. orange juice
2 tsp. sugar
1 tsp. grated fresh orange peel
   (zest)
3 tbs. butter, melted
¼ cup hot water

1½ cups bread cubes
⅓ cup chopped toasted pecans
3 tbs. raisins
¼ tsp. salt, or more to taste
⅛ tsp. cinnamon
pepper to taste
1 tbs. butter, melted
2 tsp. Kitchen Bouquet
2 Rock Cornish game hens
   (about 1¼ lb. each)

Preheat oven to 450°. In a heavy saucepan, place cranberry sauce, orange juice, sugar and orange peel. Cook over medium heat, stirring constantly, until it begins to boil. Remove from heat and cool completely. In a bowl, mix together 3 tbs. butter, water, bread cubes, pecans, raisins, salt, cinnamon, pepper and 1/4 of the cranberry mixture. Stuff mixture loosely into cavities. Tie hen legs together with kitchen string.

Place stuffed hens, breast side up, on a roasting rack. Mix 1 tbs. butter with Kitchen Bouquet and brush mixture over hens. Place pan in oven and immediately reduce heat to 350°. Roast hens for 1 hour, basting with butter mixture halfway through roasting time. Test for doneness by piercing a thigh —juice should run clear, not pink. Heat remaining cranberry sauce and serve with roasted hens.

Servings: 2-4

ROAST CHICKEN WITH CILANTRO-BLACKBERRY SAUCE

This unusual combination of flavors can be made tangier with a small amount of pureed sour grapes.

1 roasting chicken, 3½ lb.
¼ cup butter, softened
2 sprigs fresh thyme or tarragon, or 2 tsp. dried
salt and pepper to taste
1 cup chicken stock
3 cups fresh blackberries
2 cloves garlic, mashed
½ tsp. salt
dash hot pepper sauce, or to taste
½ cup chopped cilantro
4 tsp. lemon juice

Preheat oven to 400°. Place chicken, breast side up, in a roasting pan. Spread ½ of the butter over the outside of chicken. Use remaining butter to coat the inside. Place thyme sprigs inside bird along with salt and pepper. If desired, truss chicken with kitchen string to help keep its shape while roasting. Add stock to pan and cover bird loosely with foil. Roast for 1¼ hours, turning chicken every 20 minutes and basting with pan juices. Test for doneness by piercing a thigh with a knife — juice should run clear, not pink. Remove chicken from oven and rest for 15 minutes before carving into serving pieces.

Puree berries with a blender and strain through a sieve. Add remaining ingredients and stir to combine. Taste and adjust seasonings. Serve at room temperature with chicken.

Servings: 4-6

CHICKEN BREASTS WITH BLUEBERRY SAUCE

Interesting flavors combine to make a simple, but unique, dish.

1½ cups chicken stock
¼ cup red currant jelly,
   or to taste
2 tsp. raspberry vinegar
1 tbs. cornstarch mixed with
   1 tbs. water
1 cup blueberries

flour for dredging
salt and pepper to taste
6 boneless chicken breasts,
   skinned and cut into 1-inch
   strips
2 tbs. butter
2 tbs. vegetable oil

    Place stock, jelly and vinegar in a saucepan and bring to a boil. Add cornstarch mixture and stir until mixture begins to thicken. Add blueberries and cook for 5 minutes. Add seasonings. Keep warm. Mix flour with salt and pepper. Dredge chicken strips in flour mixture. Fry in butter and oil until golden brown. Serve warm with sauce.

Servings: 6

CLASSIC CRANBERRY SAUCE

*Thickening this sauce with cornstarch yields a texture
reminiscent of canned cranberry sauce. It goes well with
poultry or pork dishes.*

1 lb. (4 cups) fresh or frozen cranberries
1½ cups sugar
2 cups water
1 tbs. cornstarch mixed with 1 tbs. water, optional

Place cranberries, sugar and water in a saucepan and bring slowly to a boil. Cover and cook over low heat for about 10 minutes or until berries burst. (If you desire a thicker sauce, add cornstarch before cooking.) Remove from heat and cool to room temperature. Refrigerate until ready to use. If you prefer a smooth sauce, puree mixture with a food processor or blender.

Makes: 4 cups

CURRIED CRANBERRIES

This dish is great alongside poultry dishes or as a spread on turkey, chicken or pork sandwiches. It makes a nice gift in a decorative jar.

1 pkg. (12 oz.) fresh cranberries
water to cover
1½ cups sugar, or to taste
2 tbs. mango chutney
1 cup chopped toasted pecans
2 tsp. curry powder

Place cranberries in a saucepan and cover with water. Add sugar and cook over medium heat until berries begin to split. Remove from heat and cool. Stir in remaining ingredients, taste and adjust seasonings. Store in the refrigerator until ready to use.

Makes: 4 cups

CRANBERRY CRUNCH

*Use **Classic Cranberry Sauce**, page 37, or canned. Toasting the nuts gives them extra crunch.*

1½ cups graham cracker
   crumbs
½ cup sugar
1 tsp. cinnamon
½ cup chopped toasted walnuts

⅓ cup butter, melted
3 cups cranberry sauce
1½ tbs. grated fresh orange
   peel (zest)
whipped cream for garnish

Preheat oven to 350°. In a bowl, combine graham cracker crumbs, sugar, cinnamon, walnuts and melted butter. Press ⅔ of the crumb mixture in the bottom of a greased 8-inch square pan. Mix cranberry sauce with orange peel and spread evenly over crust. Sprinkle with remaining crumb mixture and bake for 30 minutes. Serve warm with a large dollop of whipped cream.

Servings: 9

BERRY BETTY

You can use this as a basic recipe for any type of berries such as blueberries, blackberries, loganberries or a combination. Serve it with a dollop of whipped cream or ice cream, or in a pool of lemon sauce, vanilla cream sauce or even hard sauce.

2 cups fresh breadcrumbs
1/3 cup butter, melted
2 1/2 cups berries
1/2 cup sugar, or to taste
cinnamon or nutmeg to taste
1/2 cup chopped toasted nuts
1/2 cup water
2 tbs. lemon juice
1 tbs. grated fresh lemon peel (zest)

Preheat oven to 350°. In a bowl, mix breadcrumbs with butter. Sprinkle a 1½- to 2-quart baking dish with ⅓ of the breadcrumbs, cover with ½ of the berries and sprinkle with ½ of the sugar, spices and nuts. Repeat layers. Top with remianing crumbs. Mix water, lemon juice and peel together and pour over dish. Bake for 45 minutes. If the top is browning too fast, cover with foil and continue baking.

Servings: 6

BERRY COBBLER

*A cobbler consists of a rich biscuit dough that is baked over fruit.
The amount of sugar used depends on the tartness of the berries.
Serve it with vanilla ice cream or whipped cream.*

6 cups fresh berries
1½ cups sugar, or to taste
2 tbs. flour
2 tbs. butter, cut into pieces

Preheat oven to 425°. Grease a 9-x-13-inch pan. Place berries,
sugar and flour in a saucepan and heat to a boil. Reduce heat and
simmer, stirring, until mixture thickens. Remove from heat and pour
into greased pan. Dot fruit mixture with butter.

TOPPING

1¾ cups sifted flour
1 tsp. salt
1 tbs. baking powder
2 tbs. sugar
¼ cup butter, cut into pieces
¾ cup milk or cream
¾ tsp. cinnamon

Mix flour, salt, baking powder and sugar together in a bowl. Cut butter into mixture with a pastry blender or 2 knives until it resembles coarse meal. Stir in milk or cream until blended and drop by table-spoonfuls onto berry mixture. Sprinkle top of dough with cinnamon. Bake for 30 minutes, or until dough is lightly browned and cooked throughout. Serve warm.

Servings: 12

BERRY CRISP

Use this general recipe for any type of berry or a combination. If berries are very tart, sprinkle with additional sugar before topping.

4 cups berries
1/4 cup butter
1/2 cup flour
1 cup brown sugar, packed
1/2 tsp. cinnamon
1/2 tsp. nutmeg
1/4 tsp. salt

Preheat oven to 375°. Place berries in a greased 9-inch pie plate or square baking pan. In a bowl, combine remaining ingredients until mixture resembles coarse meal and sprinkle over berries. Bake for 30 minutes. Serve warm.

Servings: 6

DESSERTS

STRAWBERRY AND COCONUT CREAM

This simple dessert can be thrown together in minutes.

1 qt. strawberries
1 cup sweetened condensed milk (can use low-fat)
⅓ tsp. salt
2 tbs. lemon juice
1½ cups pineapple juice
2 cups shredded toasted coconut

Wash, hull and slice strawberries and place in a shallow serving dish. In a bowl, mix sweetened condensed milk, salt, lemon juice and pineapple juice together and spread over strawberries. Chill for several hours. Top with toasted coconut just before serving.

Servings: 8

STRAWBERRY CRUNCH CAKE

Try this cake warm with ice cream. It's also good for breakfast.

2 cups flour
4 tsp. baking powder
1/3 cup sugar
3/4 tsp. salt
1/3 cup butter, cut into pieces
2/3 cup milk
1 egg, beaten
2 cups sliced fresh strawberries
1/2 cup sugar

Preheat oven to 425°. Mix together flour, baking powder, ⅓ cup sugar and salt. Cut in butter with a pastry blender or 2 knives until it resembles cookie crumbs. Mix together milk and egg and stir into flour mixture, mixing well. Spread mixture in a greased 9-x-13-inch pan, cover with strawberries and sprinkle with ½ cup sugar.

TOPPING

¼ cup butter
¼ cup sugar
½ cup flour

Mix together butter, sugar and flour. Sprinkle over berries. Bake for 35 to 40 minutes.

Servings: 8

BLUEBERRY STREUSEL CAKE

Huckleberries can be substituted or mixed in with the blueberries.
Sour cream makes this cake moist and slightly tangy.

2¾ cups flour
1½ tsp. baking powder
1½ tsp. baking soda
1 tsp. salt
¾ cup butter, softened
1 cup sugar
3 eggs
2 cups sour cream (can use low-fat or nonfat)
2 tsp. vanilla extract
1 cup brown sugar, packed
1 cup chopped toasted walnuts
1 tsp. cinnamon
2 cups blueberries

Preheat oven to 350°. Grease and flour a tube pan or Bundt pan. In a bowl, combine flour, baking powder, baking soda and salt. With a mixer, beat butter and sugar until fluffy. Add eggs one at a time, beating well between additions. Mix sour cream and vanilla together and add to butter mixture alternately with flour mixture. Mix until a smooth batter is formed.

In a separate bowl, mix brown sugar, walnuts and cinnamon together. Reserve ½ cup of the mixture and stir remaining mixture into blueberries. Spread ⅓ of the batter in prepared pan and sprinkle with ½ of the berry mixture. Repeat procedure, ending with remaining ⅓ of the batter. Sprinkle top with reserved streusel mixture. Bake for 60 minutes, or until a knife inserted in the cake comes out clean. Cool for 10 minutes before removing from pan.

Servings: 12

PAVLOVA

If you wish, you can make this beautiful dessert into small individual rounds. Substitute any type of berry for the blueberries.

6 egg whites
1/8 tsp. salt
1/2 tsp. cream of tartar
6 tbs. cold water
2 tsp. white vinegar
2 tsp. vanilla extract
2 tbs. cornstarch

2 cups superfine sugar
2 cups whipping cream
2 bananas, peeled and sliced
1 pt. strawberries, hulled and sliced
1 pt. blueberries
3 kiwi, peeled and sliced

Preheat oven to 300°. Draw 4 circles on a sheet of parchment paper with the following diameters: 10 inches, 8 inches, 6 inches and 4 inches. Grease parchment well and place on a cookie sheet.

With a mixer, beat egg whites until foamy. Add salt and cream of tartar and beat on high speed until stiff. Add water, vinegar, vanilla,

cornstarch and sugar and beat for 10 minutes, until mixture resembles marshmallow cream. Spread meringue evenly over each circle, building up the sides in a bird's nest shape. Place in a 300° oven and bake for 45 minutes or until very dry and crisp, but not brown. Turn off oven and dry meringues, with the door closed, for several hours.

To assemble, carefully remove 10-inch meringue from parchment and place on a serving platter. Spread a thick layer of whipped cream over meringue and cover with banana slices. If desired, place a few strawberries around the edges for color and center 8-inch meringue on top. Spread a thick layer of whipped cream on 8-inch meringue and sprinkle with blueberries. Repeat procedure with 6-inch meringue, using kiwi, and 4-inch meringue, using strawberries. Serve immediately.

Servings: 12

RASPBERRY TIRAMISU

*Raspberries add a new dimension to this very popular dessert.
Marsala is a fortified sweet wine from Italy. Mascarpone is a very
rich Italian double cream cheese. It can be found in specialty
stores and many grocery stores.*

15 egg yolks
1¼ cups Marsala wine
1¼ cups sugar
1 lb. mascarpone cheese
1¾ cups whipped cream
2 cups brewed espresso
¼ cup sugar
⅛ cup brandy
1 lb. ladyfingers
2 cups fresh raspberries
grated semisweet chocolate for garnish

Whisk together egg yolks, Marsala and 1¼ cups sugar in the top of a double boiler. Stir over boiling water until mixture thickens, about 10 minutes. Remove from heat and immediately stir in mascarpone cheese until it melts. Cool to room temperature; when cool, gently fold in whipped cream.

In a saucepan, mix espresso and sugar together. Stir over medium heat until sugar is dissolved. Remove from heat and add brandy. Dip ladyfingers in espresso mixture and line the bottom of a 9-x-5-inch loaf pan with dipped ladyfingers. Spread ½ of the egg yolk mixture over ladyfingers and sprinkle with ½ of the raspberries. Repeat procedure. Garnish with a sprinkling of grated chocolate. Refrigerate until ready to serve and slice into serving pieces.

Servings: 8

RASPBERRY SORBET

*This nonfat dessert is ideal for spring or summer meals. Serve it
with a sprig of mint, a few fresh berries and a crisp cookie.
Increase the amount of sugar if you use frozen berries.*

8 cups fresh raspberries
6 tbs. lemon juice
pinch salt
1⅓ cups superfine sugar, or to taste

Puree raspberries with a food processor or blender until smooth.
Strain through a fine sieve to remove seeds. Add remaining ingredients, taste and adjust seasonings. Freeze in an ice cream maker
according to manufacturer's instructions. Keep frozen until ready to
serve.

Servings: 10-12

CRANBERRY MANDARIN SORBET

Serve this cool treat as a palate refresher or a light dessert.

²/₃ cup superfine sugar
²/₃ cup water
1 pkg. (12 oz.) fresh cranberries
2 tbs. chopped fresh orange
   peel (zest)

4 cans (11 oz. each) Mandarin
   orange segments, drained
2 tbs. orange liqueur
cranberries and Mandarin
   orange segments for garnish

Boil sugar and water together until sugar dissolves. With a food processor or blender, process cranberries, peel, orange segments and liqueur until finely chopped. Add to sugar mixture and pour into a 9-x-13-inch pan. Freeze for several hours or overnight. Process mixture with a food processor or blender until slushy. Freeze. Process again for a smoother sorbet. Let sorbet sit at room temperature for about 10 minutes before serving.

Servings: 12

DESSERTS

CUSTARD CREAM BERRIES

This makes a wonderful summertime dessert, or it can be served as a special breakfast treat.

2 eggs
½ cup sugar
1 tbs. flour
1 tsp. grated fresh lemon peel
   (zest), optional

2 tbs. lemon juice
1 cup pineapple or orange juice
2 cups whipping cream,
   whipped
2 pt. mixed fresh berries, hulled

In a heavy saucepan, mix together eggs, sugar, flour, lemon peel, if using, lemon juice and pineapple juice. Bring to a boil, reduce heat and simmer, stirring constantly, until mixture thickens. Remove from heat, cool completely and stir in whipped cream. Refrigerate until ready to serve. To serve, place berries in individual serving dishes and spoon custard on top.

Servings: 6

BERRY BRULÉE

This "quick fix" dessert can be nonfat if you use nonfat sour cream. For great color and taste, combine several varieties of berries such as raspberries, blackberries, blueberries, strawberries, or any type that suits your fancy.

3 cups fresh berries
1 cup sour cream
1 tsp. vanilla, almond or berry extract
1 cup brown sugar, packed

Preheat broiler. Place berries in a shallow ovenproof dish. Mix sour cream and extract together and pour over berries. Sprinkle brown sugar over sour cream mixture and place under broiler. Broil until sugar caramelizes, taking care not to burn. Cover and refrigerate until ready to serve.

Servings: 4-6

RASPBERRY PIE

The crust recipe makes a double crust, so wrap the remainder of the dough and freeze it for another use. Serve this luscious pie with a dollop of whipped cream or vanilla ice cream. Framboise is a clear, sweet raspberry liqueur.

BASIC PIE CRUST

2 cups flour, sifted
¼ tsp. salt
3 tbs. shortening, chilled

¾ cup cold butter, cut into
    pieces
⅓ cup ice water

Stir together flour and salt. With a pastry blender or 2 knives, blend in shortening and butter until mixture resembles coarse meal. Stir water into flour mixture; quickly form into a ball. Divide dough in half and flatten each half into a disk. Cover with plastic wrap and refrigerate for 1 hour. (Freeze remaining half if not using.) Preheat oven to 450°. Roll out dough to a 10-inch round. Line a 9-inch pie plate with

dough and crimp edges. Line pastry with parchment or foil and fill with dried beans or pie weights. Bake for 12 minutes, remove from oven and reduce temperature to 400°. Remove beans and parchment and return crust to oven. Bake for about 8 minutes, or until crust is golden brown. Cool.

FILLING

9 cups fresh raspberries
2 tbs. water or framboise
1 cup sugar

3 tbs. cornstarch
1½ tbs. butter

Puree ½ of the berries with a blender. Pour into a saucepan with water and bring to a boil. Strain through a sieve and return to saucepan. Add sugar and cornstarch and boil for 1 minute, stirring constantly. Remove from heat and stir in butter. Cool to room temperature. Place remaining berries in crust and pour in cooled berry mixture. Refrigerate until ready to serve.

Servings: 6-8

STRAWBERRY PIE

This is a fantastic dessert, especially when strawberries are at the peak of their season. An almond crust gives this pie its special crunchy texture. If desired, serve with a dollop of whipped cream.

CRUST

1 cup finely chopped almonds
1/2 cup unsalted butter, softened
2 tbs. sugar
1 1/2 cups flour
1/2 egg, beaten
3/4 tsp. almond extract

Preheat oven to 350°. Mix all ingredients together until well blended and press in a 9-inch pie pan. Chill in the refrigerator for 20 minutes. Bake for 18 minutes or until crust is golden brown. Cool completely before filling.

FILLING

¼ cup almond paste, optional
1½ cups cold water
1½ cups sugar
6 tbs. cornstarch
6 tbs. strawberry gelatin
4 cups strawberries, hulled

If desired, spread almond paste on the bottom of cooled crust. In a saucepan, combine water, sugar, cornstarch and gelatin and bring to a boil. Reduce heat to medium and cook, stirring constantly, until mixture thickens. Remove from heat and cool for 10 minutes. Cut large strawberries in half. Mix strawberries with gelatin mixture and pour into crust. Refrigerate for several hours before serving.

Servings: 8

DESSERTS

GOOSEBERRY PIE

Gooseberries are not always easy to find, but it's worth the effort when made into this delicious pie. Blueberries can be substituted or added to the gooseberries if you are unable to find enough.

4 cups fresh gooseberries, stemmed
2 cups sugar
¼ cup cornstarch or arrowroot
½ tsp. cinnamon
¼ tsp. mace or nutmeg
¼ tsp. salt
Basic Pie Crust, page 58, unbaked
2 tbs. butter, cut into small pieces
whipped cream or ice cream for garnish, optional

Preheat oven to 450°. Place gooseberries in a bowl with sugar, cornstarch, cinnamon, mace and salt. (If gooseberries are very large, cut them in half.) Line a 9-inch pie plate with bottom crust. Pour gooseberry mixture into crust and dot with butter. Place top crust over filling. Trim crust to 1 inch from the edge of pie plate, fold crust under bottom crust and flute edges. Cut a few slits in top crust to allow steam to escape and bake for 10 minutes. Reduce heat to 350° and bake for 1 hour, until crust is golden brown. If desired, serve with a dollop of whipped cream or ice cream.

Servings: 6-8

BERRY JAMS

Listed below are general instructions for making a variety of berry jams. Each formula is based on 3 qt. berries and 1 pkg. (1¾ oz.) dried pectin, if called for. Some berries have enough natural pectin to "gel" naturally. Experiment with different amounts of pectin to determine your ideal recipe.

Blackberries: pectin, 8 cups sugar, ¼ cup lemon juice
Blueberries: pectin, 6 cups sugar, ¼ cup lemon juice, pinch mace, optional
Boysenberries: pectin, 8½ cups sugar
Gooseberries: pectin, 8 cups sugar
Huckleberries: pectin, 8-10 cups sugar, ¼ cup lemon juice
Loganberries: pectin, 8½ cups sugar
Raspberries: pectin, 8½ cups sugar
Strawberries: 8½ cups sugar, 3 tbs. lemon juice, 1 tbs. butter

GENERAL INSTRUCTIONS

1. Place washed berries in a heavy saucepan. Crush the lower layers to produce a little juice so berries won't burn when cooked. If there doesn't seem to be enough juice, add ½ cup water.

2. Stir in pectin, if using.

3. Simmer fruit uncovered until soft.

4. Add sugar and stir until dissolved.

5. Bring mixture to a boil and continue to stir to avoid sticking and/or scorching. Reduce heat and cook, uncovered, until thickened, for up to 30 minutes. Remove from heat and skim foam, if necessary. Add flavorings such as lemon juice or butter, if called for.

(please turn page for canning and processing instructions)

6. Sterilize canning jars by boiling them in water for 15 minutes. Remove and air dry.

7. Carefully ladle jam into warm jars leaving a ⅛-inch wide space at the top. Wipe rims thoroughly. Position canning lids and screw on bands securely.

8. Submerge jam-filled jars in in boiling water for 10 minutes. (Note that high altitude may change processing time.) Remove jars from water and cool for at least 12 hours.

9. Check lids for a proper seal by pressing the center. If it springs up, reprocess jam with a new lid before cooling.

10. Store jam in a cool, dry, dark area.

Makes: 7-10 (8 oz.) jars

BERRY YOGURT SHAKE

This shake makes a great breakfast drink or a refreshing after-school treat. Use cold ingredients for a thicker, more invigorating drink. Use marionberries, blueberries, raspberries, loganberries, strawberries or a combination.

2 cups plain or fruit yogurt
1/2 cup milk
1 cup berries
1 tsp. vanilla extract
pinch nutmeg, mace or cinnamon
sugar, brown sugar, honey or maple syrup to taste, optional

Place all ingredients, except sweetener, in a food processor or blender container and process until smooth. Taste, add sweetener, if desired, and whirl for 30 seconds.

Makes: 3 1/2 cups

CRANBERRY BISHOP

Mixed berries can be used in this Northern European mulled wine.

1 lb. (4 cups) fresh cranberries
1 bottle (750 ml) sweet white wine
one 4-inch cinnamon stick
1/2 cup sugar
2 tbs. lime juice
1/2 cup brandy

Place 1 cup of the cranberries, 1 cup of the wine, cinnamon stick and 1/4 cup of the sugar in a saucepan and simmer for 10 minutes. Remove cinnamon and puree mixture with a blender. Return mixture to saucepan, add remaining sugar and lime juice and cook for 3 minutes. Cook remaining cranberries in 1 cup of the wine for 5 minutes, or until tender. Combine all ingredients. Serve hot or cold.

Servings: 6

STRAWBERRY SAUCE

This sauce is a great topping for ice cream or other desserts, such as cheesecake.

2 cups sliced fresh strawberries
1/4 cup strawberry jam, or more to taste
1 tsp. lemon juice

Place all ingredients in a heavy saucepan and stir over medium-low heat until strawberries are softened. Add more jam if you prefer a sweeter sauce. Refrigerate until ready to use.

Makes: 2 cups

HOT RASPBERRY BUTTER SAUCE

Serve this delicious sauce over dessert soufflés, bread puddings and dessert puddings, or even for breakfast on a fluffy omelet or waffles.

1 pt. fresh raspberries
½ cup dry white wine
¼ cup sugar, or to taste
1 cup unsalted butter, cut into pieces

In a small saucepan, heat raspberries and wine to a boil. Reduce heat to medium and cook for about 15 minutes, stirring occasionally, until thickened. Remove from heat and puree with a food processor or blender. Add sugar. Return puree to pan and whisk in butter a little at a time. Strain mixture through a sieve and serve immediately.

Makes: 2 cups

CRANBERRY-APPLE SAUCE

This is good to serve with pork meals, on roast turkey, for break-fast, as dessert by itself, or over ice cream or pound cake. Use Golden Delicious, Granny Smith or Pippin apples.

2 cups fresh cranberries
2 cups sliced apples
$\frac{3}{4}$ cup water
1 cup sugar, or to taste

Combine all ingredients in a saucepan. Cook over medium heat, stirring occasionally, until fruit is tender, about 20 minutes. Remove from heat and cool slightly. For a smooth sauce, puree with a food processor or blender.

Makes: 4 cups

BLUEBERRY SAUCE

Use this great sauce in place of syrup for pancakes or waffles.
Also, consider using it as a topping for ice cream or over desserts.
Add 1 to 2 tbs. vinegar and make a sauce to accompany
strong-flavored meats like game meat or duck.

1 qt. sweetened grape juice
3-4 tbs. cornstarch or arrowroot
⅓ cup honey
2 cups fresh or frozen blueberries

In a large saucepan, mix together grape juice, 3 tbs. cornstarch and honey. Heat to a boil. Reduce heat to medium and stir until mixture thickens. (If you prefer a thicker sauce, mix remaining 1 tbs. cornstarch with 1 tbs. water and add to saucepan, stirring until mixture thickens.) Remove from heat and stir in blueberries.

Makes: 6 cups

GOOSEBERRY SAUCE

This sauce goes nicely with fish and poultry dishes. The sweetness of the berry can vary considerably.

1 lb. green gooseberries,
   stemmed
boiling water to cover
2-4 tbs. sugar, or to taste
½ cup butter

⅓ cup flour
2 cups hot water
salt and pepper to taste
pinch nutmeg, or to taste
pinch anise or fennel, or to taste

Place berries in a saucepan and cover with boiling water. Simmer gently until berries turn yellow. Puree berries with a food processor or blender and strain through a sieve. Add sugar. In a saucepan, melt ½ of the butter, stir in flour and cook for about 30 seconds. Add hot water and stir until thickened. Stir remaining butter into sauce a little at a time. Stir in gooseberry puree and seasonings. Serve warm.

Makes: 3 cups

CRANBERRY PAN GRAVY

This is great with roasted poultry and pork dishes.

1 bag (12 oz.) fresh or frozen
   cranberries
¾ cup sugar, or to taste
scrapings from roasting pan,
   optional

1 cup water, optional
¼ cup butter or pan drippings
¼ cup flour
4 cups turkey or chicken stock
salt and pepper to taste

In a saucepan, cook cranberries and sugar over medium-low heat, stirring frequently, until berries begin to burst. Puree berries and set aside. If using pan scrapings, drain excess oil from roasting pan. Add water and stir to scrape up the browned bits. Simmer for about 5 minutes. In a saucepan, melt butter and stir in flour until a paste forms. Stir in stock and contents of roasting pan, if using. Stir over medium heat until thickened. Stir in salt, pepper and cranberries.

Makes: 5 cups

BLACKBERRY BUTTER SAUCE

This rich, buttery sauce is ideal for fish or fowl. Small wild blackberries make the sauce especially good.

1½ cups blackberries
3 oz. balsamic vinegar
3 oz. dry white wine
½ cup finely minced onions
dash white pepper
3 cups butter, cut into pieces
sugar to taste, optional

Puree blackberries with a food processor or blender and sieve to remove seeds. In a saucepan, heat vinegar, wine, onions and pepper. Cook until mixture reduces by ½. Slowly whisk in butter, a few pieces at a time. Stir in puree and sweeten if desired. Serve immediately.

Makes: 4 cups

INDEX